THE HISTORY OF THE ABERDEEN STREET FELLOWSHIP CHOIR AND MUSICIANS

Christian Mentoring Stories
from Peel Street to Aberdeen Street
1976 – 2006

THE HISTORY OF THE ABERDEEN STREET FELLOWSHIP CHOIR AND MUSICIANS

Christian Mentoring Stories
from Peel Street to Aberdeen Street
1976 - 2006

S KAY OLIVER

Glasso Afoofa Publishing

CONTENTS

Acknowledgements

I thank God first of all for giving me the strength and opportunity to conduct this research and write this important book.

The findings of this research serve as a strong reminder of the positive impact that this gospel choir has made and is continuing to make on the spiritual, personal and social development of individuals of all ages, but particularly the young people.

Throughout the research, development, writing and publishing of this book, I worked with a large number of people who co-operated and supported me in many ways. I would like to express my appreciation to them all. To those named in the book, thank you for giving permission.

I would like to give a huge vote of thanks to the choir, the directors, musicians, technical support team, the churches, the community and all who participated in, and assisted with, this research.

I would like to thank Lorraine Oliver for advice and support with the revision of one choir leader's section and to Charmain Oliver for checking through the book.

Special thanks to Bishop Basil Richards, Pastor Charles Matthews, Pastor Lawrence Telfer, the ministerial team and all the members at Aberdeen Street Church of God of Prophecy for praying for me and supporting me.

Thank you to the mothers and fathers who pray for me without ceasing. I applaud and appreciate you as my prayer warriors. Keep praying those prayers.

I appreciate and love my father Herville Emanuel Jackson for all his words of encouragement and advice to trust in God. Thanks to all my family members, especially James Nolan for administrative support.

Finally, I would like to say how grateful I am to my dear husband and best friend George, our children, Lydia, Simon and Adam for giving up family time to consistently support me during the research and writing of this book.

S Kay Oliver
June 2007

Foreword

A year from the day that I wrote this book, God brought me back to a revelation that He gave to me regarding the circle and cross in the Church of God of Prophecy at Aberdeen Street. The revelation was that the circle represents the earth and the four open corners represent the four corners of the earth from where the people will come. God is saying, return from all four corners – north, south, east and west. The cross is empty because Christ is no longer hanging on the cross but the cross is the symbol of his death and resurrection. Three decades have closed for this Choir and the fourth is now open. There is a section of the circle that is cut off, saying that part of the world is cut off, severed. The cross moves to cover the outer space. Therefore those people who are considering living or taking journeys into outer space are covered and called to return to the foot of the cross. The world is in sections, cut with open access, for the people to get through to the cross. The cross is on top of the world, showing the superior power of God over the world. This is the house of God. This is a sign to remind my people that I am God. The wood represents an element that can be destroyed by judgement of fire. The warning comes to return before the day of judgement. The call is to go into the entire world. Take the sound of the trumpet to the four corners of the earth and beyond to return the people to the foot of the cross. Thus, said the Lord God of heaven, the time is short.

This revelation was received on 20th May 2006. The diary in which it was written was lost for a whole year and found on 20th May 2007. It is no coincidence that this was exactly a year later. I began working on the Choir document again in May 2007 then went to the church to photograph the cross and the circle. This all happened on the very same day God took me to find the diary. These words could not be left out of this book and I cannot offer any reason except that I must obey God.

The 'Reunion for a Purpose' concert at the Aberdeen Street Church of God of Prophecy provided the opportunity for people to turn to God. The Spirit of God led as the anointing flowed throughout the entire event. For some, this marked a new beginning. Have you found a new beginning in Christ?

God bless you as you read this book.

S Kay Oliver
31 May 2007

The Aberdeen Street Fellowship Choir & Musicians

This picture shows the cross and circle referred to in the Foreword and some members of the Aberdeen Street Fellowship Choir & Musicians. It also illustrates the recent stage and lighting improvements which facilitate better presentation.

THE HISTORY OF THE ABERDEEN STREET FELLOWSHIP CHOIR & MUSICIANS

INTRODUCTION

The accomplishments of many gospel choirs have been researched and recorded in history, some as a part of academic studies, others purely for artistic appreciation and the provision of information. However, I believe few have been studied to celebrate the value of successful Christian leadership and spiritual mentoring through singing and music while carrying out the great commission to "Go ye into all the world, and preach the gospel to every creature." (St Mark 16 verse 15, The Holy Bible). This book celebrates mentoring through worship, singing and music. It provides a historical snapshot and background to the choir, looks at how the name has changed and talks about past leaders and the present choir leader's vision. Strong leadership is very important for all choirs as well as talented and committed musicians. I will speak about leaders and musicians in this book.

Few people are still living today who can recall, with organized accuracy and in a logical way, the historical record of the past four decades from Peel Street to Aberdeen Street. It was exciting to be able to interview some of the young people from the former Peel Street Youth Choir, who came together as the Reunion Choir, for the concert in 2006. There was something special about their experiences of 30 years ago.

I have documented this small part of their history but Christ had already chronicled the story of this outstanding choir long before the seed of its inception was sown in the heart of Patricia Womack (nee McCalla) in 1976. Even before Charmain Oliver got the vision in 2005, God planned the past four decades leading up to this proclamation. The Alpha (**Αλφά**) and Omega (**Ωμεγά**) (See Note 2) knew that 2006 was the year when some members of that initial choir of 20 young people, formed in a dilapidated, pre-Second World War building in Winson Green, Birmingham, England, would re-unite to worship, minister and sing songs of deliverance. On the other hand members also will now recall, with love, and some with a hint of sadness, those who are no longer with us but whose memories live on and who will, one day, arise to tell their redemption story on the shores of glory.

THE BEGINNING - A BRIEF HISTORY AND BACKGROUND

It is important that we have an understanding of the environment and conditions that surrounded the beginning of the Peel Street Youth Choir/Fellowship Choir/Reunion Choir and some of the people that influenced the development of what we now see as an outstanding choir ministry. People had been called to come and help to "...rebuild the country..." (S Kay Oliver, 2002, p16) after the ravages of the Second World War and some only came for "five years" into an unknown territory, facing freezing winter days and nights. Among them were a group of Caribbean people who settled in the West Midlands, working in hospitals, factories and other industries, worshipping God in houses, school rooms and eventually buying their own buildings. My research revealed that it was very difficult for them to purchase a building in the early 1960s. Speaking about Peel Street, an Elder Watson said: "It was bought from either the Methodists or the Baptists because the Church of England wasn't selling to anybody at that time." One man explained that although the building looked battered, "…it was homely and it had a real pulse and vibrancy." The Peel Street Christians were motivated, creative, innovative and entrepreneurial but the most important thing to them was serving the Lord. It is within that context, and in a church bought in 1963 by Rev E L Plummer, that this story began.

The pioneering ground for this 80 plus strong Choir was a small place of worship at Peel Street, Winson Green, Birmingham, led by Christian men and women of God such as Pastor E L Plummer, Elder Crossfield and the young, energetic and charismatic, Pastor T A McCalla. Bishop McCalla summarised the amazing story of how it all began:

"It was Pat that asked me. I was living in Wolverhampton and pastoring Peel Street at the time. Pat asked me one night if I could allow her to have the young people to form a choir. I asked 'What choir do you want? We already have the church choir'. She said 'Never mind, Daddy, just allow it.' She was about 16. The church building was not good in those days. We kept repairing and repairing the windows. They knocked them out - those rough-neck children. We repaired them. They knocked them out again. Eventually we had to board up the windows and leave the boards up instead of glass. That group of young church people grew and prospered. It was not long afterwards that Bishop John Newkirt from New York visited Peel Street and preached a message on 'The Home Born Slaves'. The Youth Choir sang that evening and he commented that he was very impressed and told me that when he got back to New York he would try to start a youth choir. This encouraged me even more to support the young people to continue. It was the first youth choir in the country, to my understanding. I remember the day the Spiritual Rhythm singing group was organised by Gloria Brown. The Spiritual Rhythm was made up of Gloria Brown, Jennifer Hunter, Marcia

Simpson, Lorna 'Joy' Simmons (nee Watson), Patricia Womack (Nee McCalla), Joseph Aldred and Ann Oliver. We had the first concert at Digbeth and the whole world heard that I had backslidden because I had gone to have a concert. It was unusual at that time. Everybody thought it was appalling for me to be having a concert. I was known as a backslider - gone into the world. In Jamaica, it was the schools that had concerts. Churches normally had 'Programmes' or 'Rallies'. The first, second and third concerts, they murmured but by the fourth year I couldn't find a date to have a concert because the whole nation was having concerts. I was very pleased for Patricia's vision because a lot of churches had taken on the idea and started having youth choirs. It has worked very well. The youth were very active in their choirs in different churches. The new youth choirs from the different churches were putting on concerts regularly."

MEMORABLE RECOLLECTIONS FROM THE PEEL STREET DAYS

I interviewed a number of people who were a part of the 1970s Peel Street era. One of the original choir members revealed that the local environment was quite friendly and "... you could leave your door open and nothing would go missing." There was a vibrant Sunday School cohort. British and Caribbean children were collected from the surrounding areas for Sunday School using the two church vans and various other vans including the memorable green and cream van of Bro Campbell. One person recollects that, "...the white children came for a little while and left."

One Peel Street youngster during the 1970s, beamed with laughter as he recounted the stories of the friendly long tailed visitors that caused some young people to shriek: "The rats!" Another person described how they caused her to "...jump onto the chairs". He also recalled how the entrepreneurial teenager George C Oliver mobilised the youth to collect, store and sell old newspapers by the tonne to raise funds for the church's building programme. The kneeling pads were made in the Dorcas Club. While Bro E L Grant was preaching a "fire and brimstone" sermon at Peel Street, there was a power cut. "The people thought the Rapture had come and they started speaking in tongues." There was an expectation that Christ was coming and a thirst for the Holy Spirit.

The children felt an overwhelming sense of fun – the only small sweet shop on the corner of Peel Street teemed with the children. "After church, everybody would rush to the shop before getting into the van to go home," said one young man. Lorraine Oliver explained that: "The choir gave us something to do. There were lots of concerts at the time. It gave us a focus and it was fun. It gave you something to stay in church for. When we were at school, we did not really mix and the choir sort of brought us together." In those early days, most of the young people were at college and unemployment was high. Another choir member described the strong sense of togetherness, stating that: "There was a team spirit. They (the young people) tried everything – testimonies, preaching ..." - as part of their development.

Pauline Hines, an original Peel Street choir member, added that Lorna 'Joy' and Patricia influenced her as a young person at Peel Street. She stated that: "They were very enthusiastic and committed to what they were doing. We were very close-knit, always watching out for each other."

There was seriousness about worshipping God. People were hungry for God. Mrs Watson recalled:

> "When it was service time, they would run for the
> No. 11 bus and when the church door opened
> you would hear the vibration of the music. The

children moved in the Spirit and knocked over chairs. The chairs were uncomfortable. I usually put my children to sleep on the long bench. I would spread my coat on top of the bench and they would sleep. Our children got saved in church. I remember LB being filled at school. When the Holy Ghost took over and the chairs used to move - those were the days."

Another Peel Street choir member told me that "... back in those days, everybody helped each other ... we were together. We desired God."

The move of the Holy Spirit dominated the Peel Street era. Lorna 'Joy' Watson was saved, baptised in water and filled with the Holy Spirit at Peel Street all at the age of 7 years old. Two people from the Peel Street era gave the same account of the powerful move of the Holy Spirit: "Bro F. kicked over Gee Brown's blue amplifier as he was filled with the Holy Ghost while blessing the offering." Awesome power!

As well as a great thirst for God, there was a strong sense of discipline, and a determination to improve and move out of the rundown Peel Street building. The broken stained glass windows had been boarded up to prevent further damage by the "...rough children..." from the area. As part of the drive to generate funds to purchase better premises, a building fund programme had been planned. This would be a turning point in the founding of the Peel Street Youth Choir and its related emerging choirs.

CHOIR - NAME CHANGES FROM 1976 - 2006

During the Aberdeen Street church opening ceremony in the late 1970s, the colourful Peel Street Youth Choir marched out of their original building and into the new location as Aberdeen Street Youth

Choir. During the past four decades, the choir has developed under the leadership of Bishop T A McCalla, Bishop Wilton R Powell, Pastor Wilma Folayan, Pastor Charles Matthews, Pastor Lawrence Telfer and Pastor Basil Richards. In the year 2000 Charmain Oliver observed that the Choir included more mature parents and carers up to the age of about 50 year as well as their 12 years old daughters and sons, friends and colleagues. There was a clear theme of fellowship emerging and Charmain responded by incorporating this idea of fellowship within the Choir's name. She also recounted that: "Those over 35 were a little concerned to still be classified as youth."

CHARMAIN OLIVER'S VISION

In 2005, Charmain Oliver had a vision:

> This vision was a little "out of the box" as I call it, because it came to me like this: Look at the number of people who have been through the choir over the years. Gather as many together as you can, whether they are still committed Christians or not, whether they are in this country or area or not, whether they are still singing or not!

I thought wow, what a challenge! This vision led to the formation of the Reunion Choir.

CHOIR LEADERSHIP - PAST AND PRESENT

Over the years, the choir has been blessed with a variety of leaders and endowed with a range of spiritual gifts and talents.

First Choir Leader - Patricia Womack (nee McCalla)

Two weeks before Peel Street was due to have one of its building fund programmes, the visionary teenager, Patricia Womack (nee McCalla), had an inspiration to form a group. Sister Thompson (from the USA), once a member of the church in the UK, had visited and asked Patricia the question: "What is going on with all the young people at Peel Street?" Someone needed to harness the talents of the young people and who better than this perfectionist and strong disciplinarian. Patricia rapidly responded to this question by forming the initial choir of 20 young people. After about two rehearsals, the choir sang 'Blessed Quietness' as their first song at Peel Street. That great inspirational rendition motivated many others to join.

For three years from 1976, Patricia directed the choir with prayer, strict discipline, dynamism and enthusiasm. She commanded respect and took no nonsense. It has been said of her: "If you came late you, you would sit at the side until the next song was coming up or until the next break." Under Patricia's leadership the membership increased to 120, a remarkable achievement in such a short time, for this gifted and talented young leader. In the late 1970s, Patricia taught and directed the song "Everything Will Be All Right" and Lorna 'Joy' Simmons sang the lead to this song. Before Patricia left to marry and reside in the USA, she had already introduced the famous 4-part harmony (soprano, alto, tenor and bass - a model that had been used by the Church choir), later to become the 3-part harmony.

Patricia revealed that Sister Polly Rodney (London choir director), Sister Pearl Howe (Birmingham choir director) and Brother Millen (Wolverhampton choir director) had greatly inspired her in terms of their desire for perfection, for precision, and the care taken to get the music and notes 'just right'. God has planted in Patricia's heart a real passion for starting choirs. She not only started the original Peel Street Youth Choir but went on to start choirs in Louisiana and Georgia,

USA. When I interviewed Patricia, she said: "What God has begun, He will bring forth."

Second Choir Leader - Caroline Oliver

After the tenure of Patricia Womack, it was time for the operational sparkle of the sensitive, discerning yet strategic and observant eyes of soprano Caroline Oliver to take the choir through a transitional period. Caroline recounted: "We were all dressed in white when we sang 'Let the Church Be the Church' at Brighton Conference Centre in the 1980s." Members waved the church flag on their victory parade around the Centre. "That was a memorable occasion!" Caroline recalls the wonderful experiences in the choir, including those soul-stirring times, singing and sharing the good news of Jesus Christ in venues such as the park and outside the Birmingham Central Library; and 'backing' Jessie Dixon during his tour. According to Caroline, Jessie said he had not heard another choir interpret the song, "I am Redeemed", in the way that we had done it. What a blessing! Caroline said: "I was walking in a Mall in Cleveland, Tennessee in 1980, during my visit to the General Assembly of the Church of God of Prophecy with my brother David when I heard the singing of the song 'I Believe He's Coming Back Like He Said'. A live band was playing. It really drew me," exclaimed Caroline, her eyes glistening with excitement. "There was a revelation when I looked at the woman. She sang with conviction, vigour, meaning and feeling. She delivered a meaning that portrayed her heart and touched my heart and my life." Caroline returned with the influence of that song profoundly embedded within her heart. After listening to her sing the song, I believe the real purpose of Caroline's visit to the USA was to receive a life-time anointing to sing that song in the Spirit, using some of the highest operatic soprano notes, to re-ignite and awaken the souls of men.

Third Choir Leader - Lorna 'Joy' Simmons (nee Watson)

A change in leadership brought to the forefront the lively, energetic and exuberant Lorna 'Joy' Simmons (nee Watson), Choir leader number 3, blazing the house with such songs as "Reach Out to Jesus", a song that she had written for the Choir. Although Lorna 'Joy' may not have realised it at the time, this leading gospel choir had started taking on an international flavour, and so her attendance at workshops such as that of the African American, Mattie Moss Clarke (mother of the famous Clarke sisters from the USA) only served to consolidate the international influence. According to Lorna Joy when teaching singing, Mattie Moss was reputed to have said "Open your mouth and throw your voice to the roof." This led Lorna 'Joy' to critically analyse the effectiveness of current singing practices, particularly singing from the diaphragm. Lorna 'Joy' brought to the Choir phenomenal presence and, as a result of her training, introduced a regime of vocal exercises including tonal quality and blending. As I observed Lorna 'Joy' in rehearsals, I witnessed her excellent, God given, ability to evaluate and perfect melodic and choral compositions. There is a spiritual significance in Lorna 'Joy' being saved at 7, baptised in water at 7 and filled with the Holy Spirit at 7. After her marriage in 1990, Lorna 'Joy' moved to the Bahamas. Her choir ministry continues alongside her powerful preaching vocation. Research revealed that she has worked with choirs on an international basis including Byron Cage and Kurt Carr. In a recent interview Lorna 'Joy' said, without compromise:

> "Choirs are worshippers...who make way for the
> Word and for deliverance."

Fourth Choir Leader - Sheila McCalla

When the mantle of leadership fell on Sheila McCalla, she was also involved with the Birmingham Mass Choir. She had matured under the leadership of other choir leaders. However, she felt there was need to "...get outside of the building ... as we have a greater impact when we go out of the building." She felt the choir was a very good idea as it had the added benefit of getting young people together, the potential to support church and community and to help develop leadership skills and assertiveness. During her leadership, Sheila directed songs such as "Be Ye Steadfast, Unmoveable" and was also a lead singer. This Holy Ghost filled woman of God remembers the power-packed days of the 1970s. She recollected that although the building looked derelict from outside, "inside, the service, the power of God came down very strong." Such was the Holy Ghost pulling power that when we were in a Victory Leaders Band* service one Monday evening, the presence of the Lord was awesome "...that we came back the next day and the next day. Individuals got filled on the way home. The young people desired the spiritual things of God and wanted the Holy Ghost." Sheila was influenced by the music ministry of Spiritual Rhythm singer, Gloria Brown and J D Aldred (Now Bishop Dr J D Aldred), her Sunday school teacher at Peel Street. She felt that young people in the early Peel Street Church days "desired God" in a way that was unapologetic. "We came into the church and we wanted God. From my point of view, what I saw was what I wanted." Sheila would like to see young people develop more of a desire for God in this era and beyond, as they focus on "...ministering and being a blessing..." to themselves and others.

Fifth Choir Leader - Charmain Oliver

In 1991, Charmain Oliver took over the leadership of Aberdeen Street Youth Choir and is now the longest serving Choir Leader (15 years). Charmain had previous experience as choir leader at Handsworth Wood Girls' School and as Junior Choir Leader, along with Joanne Herlock, taught that memorable song 'Pick me up turn me around' which was Gareth Brown's solo debut. Many of the members of that same Junior Choir including Marsha Campbell (nee Aldred), Donna Telfer and Subrina Edwards (nee McCalla) are now very accomplished singers. Charmain turned her talents to singing with what became an extremely popular group in the 1980s, Clive & Co. Charmain wanted the choir to feel more a part of mainstream worship in the local church and asked if the choir could minister on the1st, 3rd and the 5th Sunday of each month to give the choir the opportunity to minister to the local church. Some of the more memorable songs that blessed the congregation on these Sundays were: "Total Praise"; "Majestic"; "My life is in your hands"; "Calling my name"; "Stand" and "Sweeter".

> "I wanted to take the choir to a different level... take the choir to do evangelism, open air meetings, out to churches not used to gospel music. My heart's desire is to see us get outside the box and stop feeling limited in our ministry and take it to another level. I see the choir as a great mentoring tool ... good for discipline... fun; ... it is exciting sharing the Word through song, and the value of Christianity is being reinforced."

This 'outside the box' vision led her to work with a range of ministries including the Assemblies of God church. Choral Fusion was an initiative involving a Hindu group, two English groups and the choir. Charmain reported: "Each leader rotated among various choirs and taught their style of singing. It was quite controversial and had never been done before. I asked God about its appropriateness then submitted it to the ministry for approval. We prayed. It was approved. We made excellent progress. The experience was warm and uplifting.

Charmain's style of leadership was very different to her predecessors. Humour, lots of laughter and correction veiled in a joke was how she got the choir members to expect more of themselves and extend their abilities. Charmain used her experience as a member of the school orchestra, and her ability to read music and arrange songs, to take the sound of the choir to another level. The musicians were reigned in. A choir member noted that "They couldn't do what they wanted any more; they had to watch the director like the rest of the choir." Charmain has a way of saying when teaching a song: "The note you are singing is not wrong, it's just not the one I want." Another said:" She has a way of correcting you without making you feel bad"

Charmain has championed the unknown singer and honed their raw talent into melodious, powerful, lead singers. Speaking about her leader, one Choir member expanded: "Charmain made us do voice training which was strange at first but then the sound that we made was different ... better". Others added: "Charmain wanted the whole package for the choir. She wants every note sung right, every time we sing to minister and perform. I think she's been really good for the choir".

"According to the Chairman, "the work of the choir is about reaching out to a wider range of people as well as reinforcing what people already know". Charmain has worked with a number of young people, encouraging and mentoring them. She continued: "The very shy have turned into bold and accomplished singers. Some may have started in the lower range in terms of vocal ability and have excelled". She has thoroughly enjoyed her time as a leader stating that: "It is fulfilling. There is so much more I want to do. I am training up the younger ones to teach harmonies". During her teenage years, Charmain grew up under the leadership of Lorna 'Joy' Watson who saw her potential. Lorna 'Joy' spoke about Charmain in an interview in 2006, saying: "I always hoped that she would become a choir leader." More recently, Lorna 'Joy' said:

"I think Charmain's leadership skills are excellent. Her ability to communicate with people is also admirable. She has earned the respect of the choir and I don't think that is easily done today, especially when dealing with young people. She has commanded their attention so she is able to bring out of them what she wants. I believe she has done an excellent job in terms of bridging the gap to bring the old and the new together. She has been able to appreciate the foundation on which this whole ministry began and certainly has the anointing to take it to the next dimension."

The choir has come a long way from the old Peel Street building. Over the years there have been small changes to the Aberdeen Street building. Charmain feels the development of the building has supported the choir: the stage and lighting has improved to facilitate better presentation. Financial rewards received for ministering outside Aberdeen Street have been used to assist in purchasing various items of equipment.

Charmain's leadership led the choir to achieve external recognition and receive accolades, including the following:

- Entry for the heats of the GMTV competition
- Winner: Radio Leicester Gospel Choir 2000
- Best Choir: Radio WM 2001
- Appearance on BBC Gospel Train
- Appearance on Songs of Praise
- Participation in the BBC Radio 4 Live Sunday morning Service 2005
- Participation in Choral Fusion – a community programme
- Performing with Jessie Dixon
- Performing at the Symphony Hall in Birmingham

Clive Anderson - Music Director/Assistant Choir Leader

Clive Anderson, Music Director, is an excellent musician specialising in the keyboard. He has been strongly influenced by the powerful ministry of his Father Leopold and Evangelist brother Fabian. "...because of their consistency and support." Clive joined the Peel Street choir as a singer and then began playing for the choir. He started as the permanent keyboard player at Aberdeen Street in the late 1980s. At times he was the only keyboard player in a musical ensemble that "...had been dominated by the guitar". As well as co-ordinating and directing all the music, Clive's role has included some management of external choir visits. He has also continued to mentor young people in the choir. As we spoke, Clive said: "Aberdeen Street was a focal point for a lot of musicians and singers and the standards just raised overnight. I would hope that I was a part of that pioneering group. For the younger people, there was a standard that was set. People like Gareth and Leon have come through and they are prodigies from the choir. What is so good is that there is healthy competition, which is done in the right way to enhance and push people to a higher level. The choir has supported me in terms of giving me a focus in church. I have made many friends. It has been a lot of fun but hard work. I have a purpose – everybody can't preach!" Clive has worked with a number of choir leaders, groups and individuals during his tenure and continues to work to develop other young musicians and singers.

CHOIR MUSICIANS FROM 1976 TO 2006

Over the years, the Choir has been blessed to have a strong network of dedicated, talented and committed contemporary musicians playing with them. This study has been an amazing journey of discovery, unearthing some of the crucial impact that this choir has had on Black musicians. Ministries have been birthed, employment has been created, doors of opportunities have been swung open, fellowship has been renewed and God will be praised. Due to limited time, it has not been possible to interview all musicians. Below is a record of interviews conducted with some choir musicians from 1976 to 2006 and also information gathered about musicians who could not be interviewed:

Alvin Ewen - Bass Guitarist

Alvin was about 12 or 13 years old when he started playing the guitar. He then switched from the regular guitar and taught himself to play the Bass guitar and the drums. As I interviewed Alvin, he said: "I was there from the beginning with people like Josh McCalla, David Oliver and David Johnson or 'DJ' as we used to call him then. We were the main musicians in church and we backed everyone in those days. We also played together in the Spiritual Rhythm, which was a gospel band vocally fronted by Joe Aldred and Gloria Brown. Also in the band were Patricia Womack, Lorna 'Joy' Watson, Jennifer Hunter, Marcia Simpson and Ann Oliver. Back in those days some of the choir songs were written by Patricia, some were written by Joy and some by both. On the original songs, all the musicians contributed to writing the music.

We played music strictly for the love of it and tried to do a good job. Nowadays, a lot of the younger church musicians play music professionally and benefit financially but in our day we played strictly gospel music and didn't consider doing anything else. We did not play for financial gain. If we got a 'pattie and a ginger beer' it was considered a bonus and we were happy to receive it. Josh was good with his hands and he would try to make up equipment at home. I remember saving up our dole money to get strings and accessories. When we did concerts, we would, if necessary, 'beg and borrow' equipment in order to provide a better sound for the audience.

Musically, those were my formative and most productive years in terms of musical training. The training was good, it was real, it was hard, it was tough, but what I learnt then stood me in good stead for when I later became a full-time professional musician. In my opinion, young musicians need to learn that playing music is a very self-sacrificial job. One needs to forget about how good (one thinks) one is and play what is required to make the song sound good instead of playing what makes the individual sound good. In addition, musicians need to work together as one unit. There is a place for each instrument when you are playing in a band situation and very often I hear young musicians playing as individuals as opposed to working together as a team. It is also very important to maintain a professional attitude at all times.

Being a musician is not just about being able to play an instrument – it is about the whole package. For example, turning up to rehearsals on time, making sure you rehearse at home privately, making sure your equipment is in good working order and having a professional and open-minded attitude. To me, it should be not what music can do for you but what you can do for the music. The reason I say that is because music touches so many people's lives, not just musicians but pretty much everyone in their everyday lives. We put on music to relax or to cheer us up or for entertainment. As a musician, I think it's important that someone should be able to put on a record that you played on, especially if it's a gospel record and be blessed by it. Back in the 1970s, there was a real spirit of friendship and camaraderie. We not only got together for church on a Sunday but we would also socialise in the week at places like the Watson's home in Birmingham and Pastor McCalla's home in Wolverhampton. Many of us even went to school together and formed relationships that last to this day. Patricia Womack spoke about Alvin as a "...perfectionist, full of enthusiasm and dedication. They gave it their best." Charmain recollects that Alvin was very enthusiastic when he was informed, over a year ago, about the Reunion Choir Concert. He agreed to play immediately. "Alvin found it quite a humbling and flattering experience to have been asked to participate," added Charmain.

Josh McCalla - Guitarist

Josh McCalla, Alvin Ewen and David Johnson were the original musicians for the Peel Street Youth choir. They also played as church musicians along with Gee Brown. Patricia Womack recalled rehearsing with Josh at home, "… so when he met with the other musicians at the church he would be able to teach them. They were the best. They were diligent and played for everybody including the Spiritual Rhythm. Josh was 10 years old when he began playing in church. The choir challenged him to continue and to remain focussed as well as giving him a sense of responsibility. At the tender age of 14, Josh McCalla was appointed as Music Director.

David Oliver - Guitarist

David played for the original choir at Peel Street under the leadership of Patricia Womack. He also played for the Spiritual Rhythm. He said: "There were other established musicians such as Bro Messam, Gee Brown and Bro John Aldred who played the big double bass. Bro Thompson played the Saxophone. Bro Berry played the banjo. He always encouraged David to play telling him that "You have long fingers, the perfect fingers for playing guitar." He was an inspiration to David. David said "I sat on the benches on many Sundays watching the other musicians play, waiting in the wings to play." After the move to Aberdeen Street, David began to play more frequently and continued to play for the choir under Patricia. The choir was very good as it gave David "…regular practice, learning new songs and new notes. The choir songs were more involved and used different techniques." It helped to develop David as a musician. Josh McCalla was very influential in David's musical career. David described him as "very gifted, very natural and he was always willing to show you how to play. If he found a nice sequence on the guitar, he would teach you how to do it, so that you could do it yourself. Josh was ahead of his time. He could make that guitar talk!"

Vindell Watson - Drummer

In conversation with Vindell, he revealed that he "had a four stringed, red and white plastic guitar" that his mother had bought for him when he was about 6. Vindell continued: "I sat down beside my mum singing and playing all the songs". Later on, Vindell joined the choir as a 12 year old and sang lead to a number of choir songs at Peel Street including "Thank You Lord". Vindell recalled that during the Peel Street days, David Oliver and George Sinclair influenced him to play the guitar and taught him his first chords. Vindell spoke with gratefulness, passion and excitement about his visits to both of these musician's homes on Sundays. He recounted: "I went home for dinner with them. Their families were kind and accommodating. After dinner, David and George would spend time with me showing me the chords. They passed that nurturing spirit on to me which I now give to other musicians. Those were very special times and, more than 30 years later, I remember those unique characteristics.

Vindell commented further that Peel Street was "…just home … just part of your life. It was what you did; it was what you knew and what you felt comfortable with. I think back to those times and for me it was special…we were just one massive family. I always wanted to run up and sit around the musicians (G Brown, David Oliver, Josh McCalla, Alvin Ewen and Raymond Grant). There was a core group of men who would encourage you to grow. They gave you the instrument to play." I believe the best way to train a young person to grow is to show them. Vindell drummed at Peel Street and Aberdeen Street.

David Brooks - Keyboard player

When David joined the choir, Hazel Watson and Tony Wilkinson were also students at Joseph Chamberlain in Birmingham, the college that he attended. David left the college to study music at Nottingham Trent University, and then returned to take up his first teaching position at the same college. David has directed the University gospel choir, Joseph Chamberlain Gospel Choir and Camp Hill Seventh Day Adventist Church Youth Choir. He conducts choral and vocal workshops in the community and is currently lecturing at Solihull Sixth Form College. According to David, "Every now and then, the Youth Choir at Aberdeen Street needed a keyboard player so I started to come here more regularly." David has been playing for the choir for a number of years and works as part of a strong and dedicated team of musicians. He regards Aberdeen Street as his adopted home.

Ray Prince - Drummer

Ray Prince is an exceptionally talented drummer who has played with the choir over many years. During an interview, Ray explained how his relationship with the choir began: "I was about 16 when I started playing for the choir in 1988. Vindell Watson had left and I took over, after Vindell and Merrick Watson, to play drums. I was playing with Robin Watson, Vincent McCalla and Clive Anderson. I left after a couple of years and Gareth took over from me, then Leon took over from Gareth. I would have liked to have played with Robin again as we were the original outfit. This would have been a real reunion for me." Responding to a question about the choir's impact on him, Ray said: "It was nice to play with one of the well-established choirs at the time. It was good profile." Ray played under Lorna 'Joy' Watson's leadership. He specifically recalls playing at 'The Cave' on Moseley Road in Birmingham. As we continued this interview, it became very clear that Ray has a deep desire to support the all-round development of young musicians. He remembers vividly, his long 2 hour journeys on the No. 11 bus carrying parts of his kit. "I did it because I loved my music. I was 17 and I didn't drive but I had to get there!" Ray hopes the support structure will have improved sufficiently to smooth the progress of young musicians as they develop.

As a result of playing music with the choir and in the church, Ray's career has developed. He is now working with a number of local authorities providing music education to a wide range of disadvantaged young people in the West Midlands region. Ray is a nationally recognised music educator and a mentor in the field of youth music, currently working on a government initiative known as "Respect".

Colin Peters - Bass Guitarist

Colin's parents, Winston and Hazel, bought his first guitar when he was 9 years old. He began playing in church from that point. Colin informed me that he played in a group with his Mum, aunt, uncle and cousins. Colin joined the choir in 1989 at the age of 16. "I was asked to join by Lorna 'Joy' Watson and Josh McCalla. Alvin had left. Joy was the leader and the other musicians were, Vincent and Josh McCalla, Vindel Watson, Michael White and Clive Anderson. It was my first experience of playing with a big choir and it was the turning point in my musicianship, playing with Josh." This experience enhanced his playing. One of Colin's other major influences was Hazel. Colin said: "She welcomed me into the choir. The whole Watson family influenced me. It changed my musical angle." Colin travelled with the choir to many concerts around the United Kingdom.

In church, the guitarist, Peter Cunningham, was an influential figure in Colin's life and remains a good friend.

Peter Daley MA BMus - Organist/Composer

Peter Daley, an outstanding organist, began playing for the choir in the 1990s. His relationship with the choir started through Charmain Oliver and Gareth Brown (his cousins). Peter said: "It's always a pleasure and a privilege to minister with the choir. Some of the musicians that I am working with today, such as Colin Peters and Ray Prince, have influenced my musical career. They were a great inspiration for my debut album, *'Apart from Life'*. I think every musician should experience playing with a choir – it's a great learning curve."

Theo Browne - Bass Guitarist

When I interviewed Theo, he said: "My father, who plays rhythm guitar, forced me with love, into picking up the bass. Although I started very late, with piano being my desire, he bought my first bass guitar and told me to play it in church. As daunting as this was, I learnt by playing along with Walter Hawkins records and the Winans Brothers. That was a part of my formative training. I then went on to pursue more formal instructions in music."

Theo has played for the Choir since 1994. He has played at various concerts and other events nationally. Theo particularly remembers the BBC Radio and the Television events, specifically "Songs of Praise" with Thora Hird, "Gospel Train" and the awards on the radio. Theo said: "Patrick Hepburn, who is also a bass player, was instrumental in my appointment to the choir. He has been a friend and spiritual brother.

Theo's main influence in his musical career is Jesus Christ the creator and focusing on the pain Christ sustained so that he can be free to worship. Theo's ultimate goal is to play bass guitar in front of the King of Kings in the New Jerusalem descending from heaven to declare his deity.

Theo continued: "In the meantime it is great to minister with the choir once again - this is a very special privilege, memorable and highly enjoyable. The experience has rekindled some special moments of those days under the direction of Charmain Oliver."

He said that he will continue to worship and play his bass guitar "as long as I have the ability and opportunity to do so".

Gareth Brown - Drummer, Percussionist & Music Director

Gareth is now a well established musician and was the main Drummer during Charmain Oliver's leadership. Gareth said: "Nothing prepares you for playing like playing in church." He lists as his most powerful influences Vindell Watson, Ray Prince and Louis Williams. "Their styles and their approach to drumming had a great impact on me" said Gareth. When asked about how the choir had helped him, Gareth commented that the "commitment has been good being part of an establishment. Even when I go away and return they always welcome me back. I have enjoyed working with the musicians and seeing how different people perceive things. I might hear one arrangement one way and they might hear it in a different way and we can combine those two arrangements to make a third arrangement."

Leon Small - Drummer

Leon joined the choir under Chairmain's leadership just before the "Calling My Name Concert" at Aberdeen Street in 1993. He joined because of his love of music. Clive Anderson as well as Gareth Brown, the main drummer at the time, encouraged Leon to play in the choir. The choir exposed Leon to different styles of music, helped to develop and improve his drumming, to learn about music and choral singing and provided the springboard to his musical career. Additionally, "...it helped to develop other skills such as communicating with other people and built character and confidence. It was another way of ministering and getting to know more about God and see God working in different ways. At 13 to 14, I had cow bells, cymbals and a tambourine. Those were my first percussion instruments. For the concert we had a drum machine. By then I had a cabassa. I used the drum machine to get other sounds and I played keyboards for the first time in the concert." Leon is now the principal drummer for the choir and is involved in the musical arrangement of songs.

Robin Watson - Bass Player

It was during Charmain Oliver's tenure that Robin Watson joined the choir. Robin said: "I was growing up seeing all the people playing in the choir - Joy was directing and Vindell was playing. I came in after Colin Peters. He was one of my mentors at the time." Colin Peters, Lorna 'Joy' and Vindell Watson were very influential people in Robin's musical life. Robin believes that, as a musician, the choir gave him a sense of discipline. "Sometimes we had to learn quite a few songs and going through that process of building the songs helped me." During his time of playing for the choir, Robin played alongside Ray Prince and they had "a great partnership." He remembers clearly, Alvin Ewen, Josh McCalla, Vincent McCalla, Vindell Watson, David

Johnson, David Oliver, Pat and Joy, as fore runners. Robin admired Sister Howe because she had a particular way of working and for the fact that she is still going now! Robin thinks it is a good idea to have organised the concert and said it enabled him: "… to catch up with a few people."

Vincent McCalla - Guitarist

Vincent has played for the choir almost every year since moving to Aberdeen Street. Vincent smiled as he said: "It is quite amazing. I remember Charmain coming as a little girl." The wife and husband team of Sheila and Vincent have worked together on many occasions.

Vincent recollects that David Oliver and Josh McCalla had a massive impact on the musicians. "David was very disciplined in what he played. Working with the musicians has been absolutely great. That is one of the good things I have really enjoyed about getting together, working with Ray, Alvin, Gareth, Colin and others. Musicians are not in competition. They are able to have a laugh. Ray is one of the best drummers in the country."

David Johnson - Drummer

David told me that he began playing drums for the Peel Street Youth Choir in 1976. During the 1970s he also played for the Spiritual Rhythm. David said: "The choir had a tremendous impact on me. It shaped the rest of my Christian life. It also had a great impact on our spiritual development and taught us what it meant to worship God and to give glory to Him."

Patrick Hepburn - Bass Guitarist

Patrick Hepburn joined the choir in 1982 as a tenor and lead vocalist. He then started playing for the choir in 1993. He felt that he needed to make a musical contribution to the choir on the bass guitar. Patrick said: "The choir has been demanding in terms of ministering to the unsaved and also in corporate worship in my local church at Aberdeen Street. I also feel that I was challenged to aspire to a higher level of musical excellence. This moved my bass guitar playing to another level. Nevertheless, I have never lost focus on the absolute and vital importance of the anointing of God and the Holy Spirit which only comes through a firm grasp of the significance of music in the body of Christ through a clear theological perspective, grounded in the Word of God. When all is said and done, with all my biblical knowledge and practical ability, it all comes to nought and my music is ineffective if I'm not first a worshiper. I'm not so much speaking of that which is seen in public but rather in private. Whenever I minister on guitar, what is heard and seen is a product of that which has impacted me through trial of faith, overcoming and the resultant shaping of character being perfected in love. First Corinthians 13 and, more specifically, verses 1-3 encapsulate this concept. My music, instrumental or not, must be clear, distinct, definable, stripped of self and personal gratification but speak truth to the hidden man of the heart - yeah the depths of the listener's inner being!"

SUPPORTING YOUNG MUSICIANS

Opportunities have arisen for young musicians to play with the choir. This is a part of the choir leaders' ongoing plan to develop young musicians.

Simon Oliver - Drummer

Music student Simon Oliver, a highly gifted young dyslexic drummer, who plans to study Music at university, has received support, mentoring and encouragement from choir leaders and choir musicians. He has rehearsed and played for the choir at one of their events in Birmingham city Centre. He also deputised for Leon Small, the principal church drummer, during his absences. Simon said that "...the choir gave me experience and the opportunity to play."

Chelsea - Drummer and Percussionist

Thirteen year old Chelsea – drummer and percussionist - has played for the choir during some of their rehearsals and deputised for Leon Small during his absences. She is described as a naturally gifted musician, who can read as well as write music. Chelsea is among a small and exclusive group of female drummers.

TECHNICAL SUPPORT

There are many faithful and dedicated technicians who have given time and talent behind the scenes to ensure sound, lighting and other equipment work effectively. The choir places value on all members of the technical support team. The current technical support team includes individuals with historical links to the Peel Street days as well as more recent choir members.

Charles Davis - Peel Street Choir Member

Charles is one of the original members of the Peel Street Youth Choir of the 1970s. He commented:

"I was very shy. I was not confident. The choir gave me confidence so I have moved on. I always wanted to play an instrument. Because I couldn't play, I sang. As a result of being involved in the choir I have gone on to work on the PA system. When we go out, I help in setting up the microphones, making sure we get the quality right."

Mark Sinclair

Mark joined the choir in 1998 under the leadership of Charmain Oliver initially singing alto then moved to tenor. Mark said: "The choir has helped me find my singing voice. You get to socialise with people that you wouldn't normally talk to. The choir has a rich sound. I am a part of the technical support team for the choir at Aberdeen Street. I am quite surprised about how long the choir has been going and how many members it has had."

CURRENT CHOIR MEMBERS SPEAK

The Youth Choir's Pastor of 1976 –
Bishop T.A. McCalla

Bishop T A McCalla sang with the Choir for the Reunion Concert. When I asked Bishop McCalla to speak about the impact the choir has had on him, he said: "They blessed my soul a lot of times ... really blessed my soul. I was in the hospital for 31 days and I had two operations in two weeks. There were tubes all over my face. I went to the bathroom, trying to clean up my face. It was difficult because of all those tubes. I began to feel frustrated and wondered how long this would be. While I was looking on my face in the mirror, as I always love to do, one of the youth choir songs just came into my mind saying 'Everything Will be All Right'. It's like I was hearing them singing "...after the storm clouds pass over, everything will be all right". That comforted and consoled me throughout my illness and years after. I sent and asked them for a tape of that song. I will never forget that. I kept humming it and I was constantly blessed by this Youth Choir. Every time I come up against something that seems difficult, that song 'Every Thing Will be All Right' comes right into my mind." As we concluded the interview, Bishop McCalla began to sing the song, and said "I could hear Joy's voice singing it all the time."

A Parent

Debbie Allen joined the choir in 1998. She had been attending the Aberdeen Street church for about a year and felt the Lord leading her to join. Debbie had sung in several choirs, large and small. She said of Charmain: "She is tenacious, very talented, committed and an inspiration. What amazes me about her is that she is still relatively young and shoulders such a great responsibility. I am impressed by that."

A Teenager

A female school pupil who joined the choir in 2005 feels it has made a big difference in her life. She said: Because I am ministering to people, it helped me to change within myself."

AN OBSERVANT CHILD SPEAKS

As I wrote, I reflected on the testimonies I had heard from many who were children of the Peel Street era, describing the last thirty plus years. This has been a miraculous God-given, God-preserved, God-protected, and God-directed continuum, where young people have grown and matured, ministries have been birthed and souls won for the kingdom. An observant child spoke about the choir and the great commission: He said of the Choir:

"I think that they are very talented and they should not stop singing for anything. Even if they end up doing it in the streets, they should carry on because I don't really know any other choir that is as good as them and God has blessed them for them to praise God just how they do it and just how they like to do it. (Blair, age 9, 20 May 2006)

Our all mighty, eternal God brought us from the 1970s Peel Street building-fund programme to the 2006 Aberdeen Street Reunion Choir Concert. He brought us from the first rehearsal on Saturday 17th December 2005 at 5.00 pm – 8.00 pm to an amazing praise and deliverance summit on Saturday 27th May 2006.

"For I know the thoughts that I think toward, you saith the Lord,
thoughts of peace, and not of evil, to give you an expected end.
Jeremiah 29 verse 11.

Notes

1. The author's understanding of some Greek words has been developed with the support of her Greek language teacher Gabriel in the Greek Class at Aberdeen Street Church of God of Prophecy, Winson Green, Birmingham, UK.

2. Αλφά (pronounced Alpha): The first letter of the Greek alphabet is called 'alpha'.

Ωμεγά (pronounced Omega): The last letter of the Greek alphabet is called 'omega'.

In the Holy Bible God is the 'Alpha' and 'Omega'.

You may wish to carry out your own research to find out more about the 'Alpha' and 'Omega'.

3. Victory Leaders Band (also known as VLB): This was a department in the Church of God of Prophecy which was responsible for young people.

References

1. Cambridge University Press, *The Holy Bible,* Authorised (King James) Version. London: Trinitarian Bible Society.

2. S Kay Oliver (2002), *A Priceless Gem.* Birmingham: Glasso Afoofa Publishing.

3. S Kay Oliver, 2006, Unpublished Research evidence for *'The History of the Aberdeen Street Fellowship Choir and Musicians'.* Birmingham: Glasso Afoofa Publishing.